For children, especially those who are still somewhat clumsy, the size of the dwarf rabbit is important, since small children can easily carry smaller pets around, and the pets, too, must be hardy enough to withstand, say, a fall, without getting hurt. The dwarf rabbit fulfills all of these conditions just fine, although its suppleness is no match for that of a cat, which is always supposed to land on all four feet.

For your children and also perhaps for you, too, the rabbit's ability to learn is especially interesting. It makes it possible to teach them tricks such as jumping over little hurdles or standing up.

And finally, there are the dwarf rabbit's features. The proportions of the head and stubby little ears, large dark eyes, and cute nose elicit a mothering urge from every sensitive person, and you constantly hear people saying "how sweet," "how cute," and so on. I've hardly ever met anyone who doesn't

These pint-sized little rabbits are every bit as appealing as their bigger brothers.

want to pet or pick up the soft, furry creature.

So, there are plenty of good reasons for keeping this small, cute animal. This book is for all who want to enjoy their dwarf rabbit pet to the fullest.

ORIGIN OF THE DWARF RABBIT —

Before I really get into rabbits and how to keep them, here's a little dry theory first. Knowing something about our little rabbit is not all that uninteresting, for you'll better be able to understand your pet once you know something about its history.

Today's domestic rabbit, the big brother of your pet, comes from the wild rabbit with the Latin name *Oryctolagus cuniculus,* which means "hare which digs underground burrows." (The allusion to hare, however, is not correct, for the hare belongs to another genus in the family Leporidae.) In the event you come across young "dwarf hares," be quite assured that you are dealing with

A wild rabbit. In coloration and size, wild rabbits look alike. Note the color of the fur, which helps to camouflage the rabbit from its predators.

WHY A DWARF RABBIT?

The dwarf rabbit's ancestry can be traced to the wild rabbit, *Oryctolagus cuniculus*. Dwarf rabbits today enjoy tremendous popularity as domestic pets.

The dwarf rabbit is a recent creation. Just about 30 years ago it was mainly the Dutch breeders who made the dwarf popular. Today, the dwarf is one of the most favorite of small pets. There are many reasons for this tremendous popularity, which makes people want a little rabbit.

Dwarf rabbits are easy to keep. Whether in the house, on the balcony, or in the garden, dwarf rabbits feel quite at home if you let them out enough and pay attention to them often. These little creatures are not a problem to feed, and don't need daily care, except of course, for a few basic things. For parents who fear great expense or loss of time, this is an important consideration.

The rabbit's relatively long life of seven to eight years, or often even over ten years, guarantees that the tearful story such as occurs with other pets is unlikely; that is, that after only two years a child has to say farewell to his playmate. It often happens that the rabbit pet bought in childhood is still around to become an old friend of its grown-up owner.

Dwarf rabbits are diurnal, like human beings; that is, they expect you to pay attention to them and play with them during the day. In the evening, rabbits, too, get tired, and children can sleep uninterruptedly, although they keep their pet in the room with them.

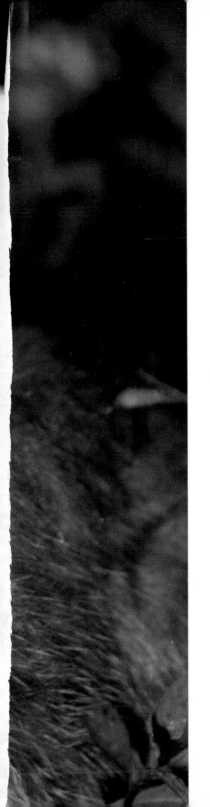

DWARF
RABBITS
AS A NEW PET

Andrea Dieker
Jutta Steinkamp

CONTENTS

Photos by Isabelle Francais, Michael Gilroy, Burkhard
Kahl, Louise Van der Meid, H. J. Richter, D. G. Robinson,
and H. Schrempp.

**Originally published in German by Franckh'sche Verlagshandlung, W.
Keller & Co., Stuttgart under the title *Zwergkaninchen*.**

Distributed in the UNITED STATES to the Pet Trade by T.F.H. Publications, Inc.,
One T.F.H. Plaza, Neptune City, NJ 07753; distributed in the UNITED STATES
to the Bookstore and Library Trade by National Book Network, Inc. 4720 Boston
Way, Lanham MD 20706; in CANADA to the Pet Trade by H & L Pet Supplies
Inc., 27 Kingston Crescent, Kitchener, Ontario N2B 2T6; Rolf C. Hagen Ltd.,
3225 Sartelon Street, Montreal 382 Quebec; in CANADA to the Book Trade by
Vanwell Publishing Ltd., 1 Northrup Crescent, St. Catharines, Ontario L2M 6P5
; in ENGLAND by T.F.H. Publications, PO Box 15, Waterlooville PO7 6BQ; in
AUSTRALIA AND THE SOUTH PACIFIC by T.F.H. (Australia), Pty. Ltd., Box
149, Brookvale 2100 N.S.W., Australia; in NEW ZEALAND by Brooklands
Aquarium Ltd. 5 McGiven Drive, New Plymouth, RD1 New Zealand; in Japan by
T.F.H. Publications, Japan—Jiro Tsuda, 10-12-3 Ohjidai, Sakura, Chiba 285,
Japan; in SOUTH AFRICA by Lopis (Pty) Ltd., P.O. Box 39127, Booysens, 2016,
Johannesburg, South Africa. Published by T.F.H. Publications, Inc.
MANUFACTURED IN THE UNITED STATES OF AMERICA
BY T.F.H. PUBLICATIONS, INC.

dwarf rabbits, not hares; the error in designation is widespread. The genus *field hare* is so different in appearance and behavior from that of the rabbit that crossmating between them is impossible, although it is often alleged to occur.

The wild rabbit is the ancestor of the domestic rabbit, even though there aren't any similarities in coloration. The "wild colored" ancestor weighs three to five pounds, which is larger than our dwarf rabbit, and is golden brown with white underparts. Wild rabbits can be found in a wide variety of habitats on most of the continents.

In the beginning, rabbits were "used" as delicious roasts, to be sure, long after the first domestic animals were around. Rabbits made attractive game, which was soon developed to the point that hunters set up permanent hunting preserves so that rabbits were always available. Since, however, hunting for meat like this was not to everyone's taste, people began to keep rabbits in fenced-off corrals—rabbit gardens—where they didn't have to be hunted, but could just be "harvested" for eating. At that point the wild rabbit type began to differentiate into various colors and sizes. Actual rabbit breeding only became possible when people started to keep rabbits in

hutches and to domesticate them. Even further differences began to separate the various groups of rabbits when they were bred for larger size and more meat. The cornerstone for many of today's breeds goes back to the Middle Ages, above all the monasteries and convents, where only the best specimens were bred.

Today, a very large number of rabbit breeds are available, from those that weigh over 15 pounds to the medium-sized rabbits and down to the dwarf breeds, which can be carried very comfortably in your arm. Your little friend belongs to these dwarf breeds. These dwarfs, of course, were not developed as a supply of meat or fur, but show the tendency of many breeders to consider the sporty look over and above any other material value. The dwarf rabbits belong to these "sport or hobby breeds," the main purpose of which is to make people like you and me happy, and not to be of any material "use" beyond that. Whoever keeps his dwarf rabbit pet properly and treats it understandingly will have a lot of fun with his new housemate. That's a value you can't calculate in money. That's why I'm thankful that the breeders of dwarf rabbits have made such a "play rabbit" possible.

CONSIDERATIONS BEFORE BUYING —

Whether you want a rabbit for yourself or for your children, you've probably already considered whether or not a dwarf rabbit will satisfy your desires and whether you can meet the requirements of being an owner. Such preliminary thought is important because our rabbit is one of the easiest-to-care-for animals and a good buy. However, you should be aware that even with a problem-free animal, a few considerations are in order before you purchase it.

Is enough space available for housing and exercise? If you live in a house with a garden or portion of one, you naturally have the ideal conditions for your housemate. Even if you live in an apartment with a patio or balcony, there is no problem. If, however, you live in a small city apartment, your rabbit should be able to run around free so that it gets the proper exercise. In that case, you shouldn't get too upset with some dirtiness, chewed rugs or furniture.

Can you pay enough attention to the rabbit? Rabbits are diurnal creatures and completely tame or trusting only if you can pay attention to them often. If you're away from the house all day or if you work, consider the possibility of keeping *two* rabbits.

Who will care for the rabbit? A rabbit is usually bought for children who have not yet had the experience of keeping and caring for an animal themselves. If, from the beginning, you let your children help in the care

6

of your little rabbit, they will learn how to deal with it very soon. No child should care for an animal alone unless he's had the proper instruction. And only when the rabbit is regularly and properly fed, the cage cleaned as needed, and the rabbit played with without being fearful or anxious, does it become a loving member of the family.

In the event that the rabbit is meant for a young child, you should realize that a dwarf rabbit, despite its sturdy body build, can seriously hurt itself if it falls. That happens most often with children under six years of age, since they are not yet capable of handling the animal in all situations. Also, the sense of responsibility necessary for caring for any animal is not yet developed enough. Here, too, the parents will have to do most of the work.

What happens to the rabbit during vacation? During vacation, the rabbit has to be left with friends or neighbors, or someone has to look in on him every other day. Although the second possibility is made easier by commercially available automatic feeders and waterers, I would still recommend leaving your pet with someone in another household; that provides continuing human contact, and any health problems can be noted at once. The temporary change in your pet's caretaker won't cause it any great distress, either. If neither of these two possibilities are feasible, then you've got to figure out another way. It's possible these days to board your pet at the pet shop where you bought it. This solution is certainly worth consideration, since you can be sure

that your pet will be cared for professionally. Ask about boarding possibilities when you purchase your pet, and then make reservations early to assure accommodations; such vacation service is rare, so accommodations are very quickly filled.

An alternative is to leave your pet in a specialized animal boarding facility. For a fixed daily price, your pet is fed and kept clean. Just as with any other business, there are disreputable places to avoid, so look in a few times and see what's going on at any boarding home you select. Then you won't have to quickly decide at the last minute whether to leave your pet at the boarding home and hope that it remains safe and sound until your

Children especially are enchanted by these delightful little rabbits. Caring for a pet will promote the young owner's sense of responsibility.

7

return, or whether to take your dwarf rabbit along with you—which is certainly a possibility.

Once all the questions have been answered and you have firmly decided to keep a rabbit, there's just the matter of accommodations to settle. Temporary accommodations for the first few days are definitely not advisable for hygienic reasons (urine-soaked cardboard boxes) and for safety reasons (the rabbit gnaws through or jumps out of the cardboard box). Your best bet is to purchase the rabbit's cage from the pet shop before you buy the rabbit itself.

Netherland Dwarf. This breed comes in a variety of beautiful colors.

SELECTION

The big day is here! The whole family is going to pick out the new family pet. The best way to find a healthy, young rabbit is to buy the animal from a well-run pet shop.

The price of a rabbit varies according to breed. A lot of price comparisons won't really help, because the rabbit you are searching for takes on its real value only when you have accepted it into your heart.

Once you've decided on the right rabbit, ask the seller to determine its sex for you, which can be important later when you consider buying a mate for your pet. The dealer can determine the sex from the distance between the genital and anal openings. Later, you yourself will be able to recognize a male from the testicles, which are clearly visible in the groin area.

Get a healthy rabbit. Find out how old the rabbit is which you select, for an animal younger than five weeks was weaned too soon and is still unable to take solid food. These little fluffballs are potential candidates for disease because they didn't get the necessary resistance-building substances which they would normally have gotten from their mother's milk. Save yourself unnecessary and futile anxiety, and buy a little older but hardly

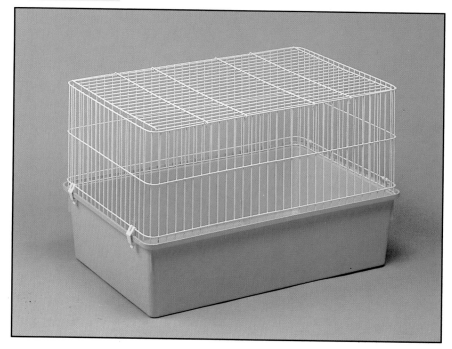

Pet shops carry a variety of different cages that are suitable for dwarf rabbits. Photo courtesy of Hagen.

less cute and cuddly six-week-old youngster.

A healthy young rabbit is lively, clean, and has a cylindrically shaped body (that is, the front part is just as broad as the rear part). The body should be compact, without any sharp corners caused by jutting bones. When your rabbit stands up on its hind legs, its forelegs are held straight and parallel to one another.

The round head seems to sit, without a neck, directly on the body. The line along the back runs in a soft arc which is not broken by jutting loins.

The claws are colorless, or brown in non-albino animals.

The cottony tail or "puff" is attached loosely to the body and carried upright.

The fur is thick and plush. If you stroke it against the grain (that is, against the direction of growth), the well-developed undercoat keeps the hairs from laying right back down again to their normal position. Stickiness and soiling on the fur of the abdomen and around the anus indicate diarrhea. A dwarf rabbit weakened by diarrhea should not be purchased.

The eyes must be clear and clean, and not runny.

A Britannia Petite. Ideally, the coloration of a Petite's coat should be as near to pure white as possible.

The nose, too, should be dry and not runny. And, above all, the rabbit should not be sneezing all the time.

Rabbit ears can be moved quite flexibly and should be clean.

Take a good look at the teeth. They should not be too long, curved or overgrown, for that would make it hard for the rabbit to eat properly.

Since you are looking for a friend and not an exhibition winner, pick the rabbit who appeals best to you personally.

Dwarf Rabbit Breeds

There are a number of dwarf rabbit breeds from which you can choose—each with a charm all its own.

11

Jersey Wooly. These adorable newcomers on the rabbit scene are gaining considerable attention in the fancy.

possible selection of dwarf-like rabbits is presented.

Britannia Petite—Petites are sprightly, energetic little rabbits with a noticeably alert demeanor. However, they can be somewhat temperamental, a quality that you may find unacceptable in a pet rabbit. Fur: fine, short, and smooth in appearance. Color: as close to pure white as possible. Ideal weight: 2.25 pounds.

Dwarf Hotot—The striking contrast between the beautiful dark eyes (each surrounded by a thin dark eyeband) and white body makes this breed of rabbit particularly attractive. If treated with regular TLC, they can be quite affectionate. Fur: a lustrous coat that is soft, dense, and fine. Color: white—pure and uniform—over the entire body. Ideal weight: 2.25 pounds.

Holland Lop—These pint-sized little fellows have retained the lop-eared charm of their larger cousins. They are, in essence, dwarf lop-eared rabbits. Some fanciers have been attracted to the breed for its loveable, good-natured expression alone. Fur: thick and dense to the touch, with a lovely, glossy appearance. Color: solid colors include pointed white, selfs, shaded, ticked and agouti. Broken colors include any color in combination with white. Ideal weight: 3 pounds.

Jersey Wooly—This appealing little rabbit has created quite a sensation with his wooly coat, and his sweet, irresistible expression has won the hearts of many rabbit fanciers. The Wooly has a short-coupled compact body and a bold, well-rounded head. Wool: ideal length is 2 to 3 inches;

Additionally, within some of these breeds there exists a lovely variety of colors and markings. Undoubtedly, your most difficult decision will be deciding just which one of these adorable little creatures will become your very special pet.

It should be noted that some hobbyists set a limit of 2.5 pounds maximum as the accepted weight for dwarf rabbits. For the purpose of this book, those breeds of rabbit that, when fully grown, weigh no more than three pounds are included in the dwarf rabbit group; in this way, the largest great density is desired all over the animal. Color: any color that is permissible in *either* the Angora breeds *or* in the Netherland Dwarf is acceptable. Broken patterns are not acceptable. Ideal weight: 3 pounds.

Netherland Dwarf—The smallest "model" available, the Netherland Dwarf is *the* favorite of many rabbit fanciers. His apple-round head, topped by very short, erect ears, sits atop a short, compact body that is wide shouldered. Members of this breed are not as feisty as other dwarf-like rabbits, and can make fine pets, given the proper care. Fur: the Netherland Dwarf sports a coat that is soft, dense and strikingly glossy. Color: within five primary groupings of coloration,

there are over 20 color varieties available. The five main color groups are: self, shaded, agouti, tan pattern, and any other variety. Ideal weight: 2 pounds.

Polish—The Polish is another very pretty breed of rabbit. However, he does have somewhat of a reputation for being high-strung and occasionally nipping at "the hand that feeds him." If you are willing to overlook such misdemeanors, the Polish can make an otherwise loveable pet. Fur: short and fine, with a glossy luster. Color: black, blue, chocolate, and white. Ideal weight: 2.5 pounds.

Other Small Rabbits
    There are other breeds of rabbit, a

Netherland Dwarfs: a Siamese sable and a Himalayan. With so many attractive color varieties from which to choose, your selection of a dwarf rabbit won't be that easy!

13

bit larger than dwarf rabbits, that you may be interested in researching before you make your final choice. The following breeds average between four and seven pounds at maturity (as opposed to the dwarf's three or less pounds): Dutch, Tan, English Spot, Florida White, Mini Rex, and Mini-Lop. These rabbits are large enough to be held and petted but are not too big (nor cumbersome) to be lifted and carried when they become adults.

Other Considerations

To be certain that the little fellow doesn't shoot up one day into a rabbit of one of the larger breeds, measure the ear length. From the base of the ear to the tip of the ear should measure less than three inches at the most. Only in this way can you be certain that your supposedly dwarf rabbit does not actually grow into a giant. Don't try to just take a chance and guess. My own attempt in this respect ended in my discovering that I had purchased (from a flea market) a young female from a medium-sized, not a dwarf, breed. Before you make off for home with your newly acquired pet, it is advisable, in the interest of the animal's health, to inquire about its food. Then you'll be spared unpleasant surprises such as diarrhea the next morning. In addition, remember that even if you've been told that rabbits don't need drinking water, you've got to let your pet have water when it eats prepared feeds. No amount of fresh food can make up for the need for water. So make sure your rabbit *always* has fresh drinking water.

14

ACCLIMATION ——

Here are a few tips on getting along with the newly acquired rabbit.

To quickly gain the confidence of your new rabbit, treat him calmly and lovingly. During the first few days at home, your new pet has to get used to his new accommodations and possibly to other family pets, such as other dwarf rabbits and guinea pigs. During this phasing-in period, you should leave your new pet in his hutch or cage, where he feels secure. You may hand him little goodies as he sits in his cage and speak softly to him, which places you in the category of "harmless," and doesn't make him anxious about being crowded and handled right away. From your rabbit's point of view, you're a highly pleasant phenomenon which hands out goodies. Sooner or later, he will come on his own accord to your hand. At that point, you can slowly scratch and pet him. If you do that slowly and gently—as you speak to him—he won't object.

Think, for a moment, of the primeval fear of rabbits, who must flee from their enemies in order to survive, and don't suddenly thrust a threatening hand down to seize the poor creature. If you do, he'll think instinctively that it's a predatory bird swooping down on him, and he'll be a bundle of nerves for a few days. To lift the rabbit from its cage, use one of the proper carrying methods; if the neck skin is hard to hold on a very young or thin animal, then use the belly-lift method. Don't subject your inexperienced young pet to too many jolting impressions when you carry him around on your arm, or when you let him run around outside. During the

If you are going to provide your dwarf rabbit with an outdoor play area, the area should be securely fenced to avoid your pet's being injured or harmed.

first weeks, avoid presenting your new rabbit to too many social encounters, for all these people certainly won't leave your pet in peace. Later, every dwarf rabbit learns how to protect himself from over-attention and being bothered, but the anxious young rabbit hasn't yet developed the self-confidence needed for that.

However, don't wait too long to introduce your rabbit to an "enemy" of rabbits, such as your dog or cat. Observe your "predator" carefully, and don't let the rabbit run free until you've clearly determined just how your carnivorous "predator" will react. If it appears—*even remotely*—that your dwarf rabbit is seen as a potential delicious tidbit, then, for the sake of your rabbit, immediately break off the "socializing," or allow it only under strict security measures. A good solution is to let your bunny have a regular daily play period where he is not in the presence of any other household pet(s).

If your rabbit gets to explore the surroundings outside of his cage, he'll mark out this "territory," just as he did his cage, by rubbing things with the scent glands on his lower jaw. By this time, his self-confidence has grown quite a bit. Then it might happen that your hopping friend gets somewhat too sure of himself and begins to gnaw on a thing or two. This problem can usually be corrected by admonishing, with stern voice, picking the rabbit up by the neck (steady the rabbit's weight with your other hand) and putting it right back into its cage.

Some rabbits may display another type of unpleasant behavior: they snap at their owner or at rapidly moving objects. This behavior is sometimes caused by offering a tidbit to the rabbit, then taking it away before the rabbit gets it. It's only right that the angry animal tries to snap at the tidbit to try to grab it, and to protect itself from being bothered. Also, when a rabbit is cornered so that escape is impossible, it can happen that this last-ditch anxiety makes him snap at his supposed tormentor or predator. This is a rare occurrence, but it's important to know why the rabbit can act that way in exceptional situations.

Angora-type rabbits. Keeping more than one rabbit will mean more work on your part, but the rabbits can be companions for each other.

THE NEW HOME ——

rabbit. It's more important than one usually supposes to have the proper accommodations ready before buying the pet. Besides the first bad impressions the new rabbit will make you have of it (because it gnaws through a cardboard box, or its urine leaks through the paper bottom of the box onto your carpet), it will also remain shy longer because it will be transferred twice in only a few days. For the rabbit, that's a new, unknown territory each time, and that frightens him.

In general, there are two different types of housing accommodations. One is the indoor cage or hutch that

All accommodation arrangements for your new dwarf rabbit should be completed before you bring him home.

Your pet will enjoy the opportunity for regular exercise.

A proper hutch is one of the most important things you can provide to maintain your rabbit's health and help him to a long, happy life. Good accommodations provide protection and a place to feed properly. The rabbit sees his new home as something like his ancestors' and wild cousins' natural warren or burrow down in the ground, a safe refuge. To approximate that at home, several conditions must be fulfilled, including placing the new home in the right location. Before we get into a detailed look at various kinds of accommodations, remember that: first the cage or hutch, then the

individuals, of course, do construct their own house for their rabbit. In both cases, you need at least a 30 x 15 inch surface area; a smaller space would hardly allow your pet any freedom of movement. The height should be at least 16 inches; the rabbit needs at least enough room to stand up on its hind legs. There's no limit on how large you can go beyond these minimal sizes.

First let's look at the commercially available styles. A rabbit home with at least a three-inch-deep, waterproof (including hot-waterproof) underpan or tray is recommended. This helps prevent problems such as odors caused by urine and the associated growth of disease-causing organisms (such as bacteria, parasites, viruses). Disinfection of the cage, which is necessary after sickness, is simple and thorough when an underpan or tray is part of the cage equipment. The recommended pan depth of three inches is determined by your rabbit's instinctive ground-scratching habits and lively hopping about, which easily scatters the litter and throws it out of the cage. Commercially available cages sold in pet shops meet these requirements quite well, and the plastic pan or tray has these necessary qualities.

The upper portion of the cage, too, differs according to make. The cage

A rabbit hutch such as this provides excellent housing for dwarf rabbits.

goes in your house, and the other is the outdoor cage or hutch.

Indoor Housing

Most hobbyists prefer to purchase a ready-made rabbit house for indoors. A variety of styles are available that have been specially designed and tested for the comfort of your pet and your own convenience. Some

A black silver marten Netherland Dwarf.

An assortment of Netherland Dwarfs: blue, black, and Siamese smoke pearl.

should not rust; otherwise, thorough cleaning would be difficult. Here's a tip to prevent rust on the particularly rust-prone bottom edges of the caging: pick a cage in which the wire screening does not extend completely down to the bottom of the pan, but sits up on a ridge or is otherwise held up just a bit from the very bottom, ground level of the pan, where moisture and hay would contribute to rusting of the cage wire. A coated wire (of non-toxic enamel or protected metal) is better than bare metal, which eventually starts to rust at the welded joints.

The cage should be closed at the top. Rabbits, especially dwarf rabbits who are in top condition, are quite able to spring 32 to 40 inches and a 16-inch-high cage is child's play for a rabbit to leap out of. The cage should open by lifting the roof screening, letting you grasp the dwarf rabbit easily and lift him out without hurting him. Be sure the cage closes securely,

for a determined rabbit can get through a halfway closed cove.

I strongly advise you not to be talked into buying special offers with a front door. Cages like that are not meant for rabbits! The rabbit is much too bulky, and can be injured when it is pulled forcibly through an opening like that.

Building a Cage for Indoors

The rabbit cage built for indoors need not be isolated and protected from outside intruders. With a little skill, a convenient indoor hutch can be constructed. It's best to plan the cage in such a way that it consists of an upper and a lower part. Basic building material is wood, suitably strong wire screen of appropriate mesh size, and roof paper or galvanized tin to waterproof the floor. The base surface is formed by the floor plate. It contains a frame of at least three inches, so that the rabbit's scratching around doesn't throw out all the hay. This rabbit home is sealed with form-fitting tin or simply with roofing paper. The roofing paper is lifted around the edges. It protects the wood from the rabbit's droppings and urine, and from its teeth. Triangular beams prevent the breaking of the roofing paper on the edges. It's advisable, too, to cover the edges with a wooden lathe; otherwise the gnawing rabbit will tear out the paper just for fun. The lathes and all other wood used in the construction must be treated to curb the gnawing urge of "Mr. Longears."

The upper part should be built from wire mesh and squared wooden beams of hardwood. First we'll set up four frames which represent the four sides. On the inner side of these frames we'll attach the wire mesh. Then the frames are screwed with wood screws onto the cage. A fifth frame makes the roof, which is fastened with piano wire and a clasp closure, making the roof open like a commercially available one. The finished upper part is simply set into the lower part. The closure to this cage has to be easy for the pet owner to open, but not for the pet. The upper part of the cage you

build can also be used in summer, as a traveling cage.

After you finish the construction job, please check your work for protruding nails and splinters. It often occurs that do-it-yourself rabbit houses look good from the outside, but on the inside reveal negligent workmanship. Both you and the long-eared lodger can be hurt from jagged edges of wire (for example, when you reach in for your pet or want to do rabbit house cleaning.) Additionally, even though you may not mind the smell of paint or wood-treatment chemicals, your little gnawer may be much more sensitive. Let freshly painted or treated rabbit housing air out a while before you put your pet in contact with them again.

Netherland Dwarfs. A well-maintained rabbit will exhibit a clean, smooth coat that is soft and dense to the touch.

The Best Place for the Cage

Purchased and do-it-yourself rabbit cages for indoor use are not enclosed spaces, so take care that the rabbit is not exposed to drafts when his home is finally in position. Rabbits can tolerate temperatures far below freezing, but constant exposure to drafts often causes colds. The proper location is light, airy and conveniently placed to allow you access to it. You should avoid keeping your dwarf rabbit in the same room with infants or sick persons, something you certainly already know.

The cage usually sits on the floor. At first, however, try to get the cage up somewhat higher than the floor so that your newly acquired dwarf rabbit can keep track of all his new surroundings and begin to develop his confidence. A tiny, defenseless creature such as the dwarf rabbit naturally gets scared when he sees unknown beings looming above, all trying to reach down and grab him. Approach your new pet from the side and about at his level until he gets to know you mean him no harm.

The Outside Hutch

Outside hutches for just one rabbit are not as available commercially as are those for indoors, so you may have to build your own. Before you decide on an outside rabbit hutch, consider the advantages and disadvantages.

Outside, the rabbit is exposed to wind and weather, so for protection from the elements, you need a solid structure, which translates into a question of expense and skill.

Your pet, if kept outdoors, will be more robust and less susceptible to disease than overly coddled indoor dwarf rabbits, which is certainly one of the advantages of outdoor housing. A grate (which should be comfortable and not so coarse that your tiny rabbit's feet keep slipping through it) in the bottom lets the rabbit sit on a clean spot while his droppings and urine fall through to the underlying tray. That also helps your housecleaning chores. You have only to empty the drawer-like tray and refill it with fresh hay, then slide it back into place.

On the other hand, there are disadvantages to outside housing for only one rabbit. The cage's location has to protect it from direct exposure to the elements. The door should not open into the prevailing wind direction (whatever that is where you live). Nor should the cage be without shade, because rabbits suffer from the heat on hot summer days. Because of their thick fur, rabbits cannot perspire well, which human beings can handle merely by shedding clothing, something rabbits cannot do. A suitable location is under an overhanging eave of the roof, which protects the rabbit from rain and direct sunlight.

Also be aware of ground conditions around the cage from season to season before you decide on a location. For example, a bone-dry place on low ground in summer can turn into a mudhole in the winter because the increased rainfall runs into the lower area, which collects the water.

In no case should the cage be exposed continually to wetness; that warps the wood and can make your pet sick. Build the cage on legs. Wrap the legs with sticky tape (sticky side out) to discourage bothersome insects. A raised cage also has the advantage of giving you access without having to stoop down all the time. Several stories or lofts can be built in for storage of feed, etc.

Stabilize the whole structure by burying the ends of the legs—the feet—into the ground; however, the wood has to be treated to retard rotting. You can tar the ends of the wooden legs or you can purchase ready-treated wood.

Your pet's outdoor cage should be located in such a place that you can get to it all year 'round. Just think, for example, about suddenly remembering having to feed the rabbit late one night at 10 pm—in the winter. Below-freezing weather can cool off any desire to feed the poor rabbit, or even to play with him. Think, too, that in 15 minutes your rabbit's water is frozen down to the bottom of his drinking pan. Glass drinking bottles freeze and burst, so warm water has to be given in the pan. Therefore, the path from house to outdoor rabbit cage should not be too long. You certainly won't feel like carrying a pan of warm water several hundred yards to an outdoor cage twice a day. Cage location is usually best right at the house. Here, too, predators won't threaten the little fellow as easily.

One last word, which hopefully won't discourage you: the structure is certainly not atrocious or ugly, but in case you have neighbors who think so, set it up out of their view.

The basic structure of the outdoor cage can be built by anyone who is handy with tools. If it doesn't seem

luxurious enough, you can embellish to your heart's content. Keep in mind as you work on your "rabbit architecture," however, that a cage more than 32 inches deep is difficult for children to reach into to pick up the rabbit.

Equipping a Cage or Hutch

Once you've set up the rabbit cage or hutch, you still haven't finished, for

A gravity-fed water bottle is ideal for providing your pet with water. Photo courtesy of Hagen.

you now have to outfit the new home with the necessary equipment.

Your little hopping friend feels

shavings, or sawdust in the "moist" corner (the toilet corner) should do nicely.

On very hot summer days, you can give your rabbit a sand floor. Otherwise, sand is not advisable because of its only slight binding capacity and its frequently unclean condition. Its very cooling effect, of course, would be undesirable in cold weather.

Feed your rabbit only from suitable feed pans. Today the practice is to use only one container for feed and a special drinking bottle (inverted bottle with gravity-fed water in a small basin), which is convenient for both you and your rabbit. The feed pan should be heavy, spacious, gnaw-proof, and easy to clean. These conditions are met by glazed ceramic bowls about two inches deep. Commercially available special bowls are characterized by great stability and durability. Please don't get the idea of using a saucer, as this would be dirtied and overturned very easily by your dwarf rabbit. Even plastic and wooden containers are unsuitable because they can be easily gnawed by rabbits.

So that feeding of dry and fresh foodstuffs is clean and simple, set a hay rack in the cage. This rack simply and effectively prevents soiling, which would be a source of parasitic infestation for the rabbit.

The amount of daily water requirements your rabbit cannot satisfy from its food has to be provided by using a drinker. Water bowls are not very suitable because rabbits take pleasure in dumping them over or dirtying them. Use a drinking bottle which, besides its hygienic

most comfortable on a soft, warm surface. He enjoys stretching out and rolling around. Droppings and urine get mixed into the bedding. To counteract this condition, the proper type of bedding material must be used.

Besides commercially available packages of sawdust, there are also peat, straw, and, by the way of exception, sand for the outdoor cage. Cat litter can be strewn in the "toilet corner" of all types of cages.

Hay should not be used because many animals eat it even when it is dirty. Straw litter alone doesn't absorb urine, so it doesn't control odors. Absorbent material such as peat, qualities, also has the advantage that it has to be refilled only every few days. Of those bottles commercially available, the best (according to my experience) is the double ball valve bottle, the only drinker that really doesn't drip. Don't buy any bottles equipped with a glass tube, because the eager animal often seizes the end between its teeth and breaks it by means of jerking back on it with unsuspected vigor. Select a drinker with a large capacity. Drinkers with a half-liter capacity are particularly convenient, and they are the ones I prefer. Smaller drinkers with test-tube shaped reservoirs are more for hamsters and similar animals. If you buy one of those small ones, you have to fill it every day.

In addition to these items, it's advisable to place a thick stick or wooden block in the cage so the rabbit can satisfy his gnawing needs on suitable objects. Particularly "delicious" and harmless are chestnut, willow, and fruit trees. This wood should not be treated because some fibers will be eaten to supplement regular nutrients, and the wrong twigs could be toxic.

For the sake of completeness, we'll mention the salt spool, which, held in a special holder, should always be among the cage accessories.

By the way, rabbits are not animals who need toys in their cage, even though they can be very playful. When

A Siamese sable Netherland Dwarf rabbit. Your pet's living quarters should be kept as clean as possible.

25

I tossed a ball into my rabbit cage, one rabbit showed only passing interest. Only my older, somewhat aggressive doe set about to systematically shred and tear it up, the only thing a rabbit can do with disturbing objects in its cage.

Outside Runs

If you're one of the lucky people who have gardens, you can let your dwarf rabbit enjoy it during the fair-weather time of the year. In addition to the possibility of leaving the rabbit in its housing outside, you can also let it run free in an enclosed area. This run can consist of either individual posts with wire strands creating fencing, or else solid frames with screening. Both kinds of enclosure can be moved about as needed and according to grass growth. Be sure to build the enclosure high enough (20 inches) and to close it. Since rabbits, as burrowing animals, excavate their own warrens, they are quite skillful at digging holes. That can lead to costly (at very least in terms of time) efforts to recapture the rabbit, so you've got to put a stop to the digging. The simplest way is to lay down a large mesh netting through which the blades of grass are within reach, but the scratching around is sufficiently prevented. So, naturally, even a well-cared-for lawn will not be disturbed, an incidental point that will relieve the anxieties of any gardening parents.

You might perhaps propose that watching the rabbit closely is another, easier solution to the digging problem. If I tell you that one of my rabbits was already hopping around outside after two minutes (just two!) of digging,

you'll agree that this solution is rather impossible. No child nor even any adult can watch a rabbit uninterruptedly without being distracted for even a few minutes.

The pet owner should be able to open the enclosure and it should protect the rabbit from dogs and other predators. A lift-up roof is the best.

Provide a refuge for the rabbit so that during its several hours out in the open it can protect itself from the weather. A rabbit run or enclosure is built only where there is grass growth, of course. Letting the rabbit sit for a long time on bare stone, such as on a terrace, because "people can see it so nicely there," borders on cruelty.

It is not advisable to suddenly let a rabbit who is used to indoor life out in the enclosure from one day to the next. The outdoor-living rabbit is, on the other hand, toughened up enough, but don't overdo it; don't neglect safeguards against break-in and don't overlook building an ample shelter in general.

The Travel Cage

A travel cage can be quite a handy item. It is basically a cage used only for a short-term stay. On one hand it serves the owner's comfort in that he doesn't have to lug his rabbit around in the unwieldy rabbit house, and, on the other hand, it protects the rabbit, who is supported by the solid walls which help reduce his being tossed around. The travel cage is used mostly to go to the veterinarian, to a stud buck rabbit for breeding your doe, or to a rabbit show. You, as a house pet owner, will usually be making only a trip to a vet, if at all. Travel cages are available commercially.

There are closed and open types of cages, the closed being more practical. Besides an appropriate floor in the cage, adequate ventilation is important. Food and water should only be put into the travel cage for long trips; water usually spills out. A travel cage can be upsetting for your rabbit, so don't subject him to it unnecessarily. It goes without saying that you must not leave a rabbit in a travel cage in a hot car in the sun.

Housecleaning and Hygiene

To help keep your bunny healthy, all cage accessories, and the cage itself, must be kept clean.

Cleaning a travel cage is necessary only after use. Housecleaning an outdoor enclosure consists only in moving it after the grass is nibbled down. Cleaning the rabbit's regular living quarters, however, takes a little more work.

Change the litter two or three times a week. Only the litter in the toilet corner has to be completely replaced; a portion of the rest of the litter can be re-used, according to how soiled it is. Use a straight-edged shovel so you can reach into the corners to clean without having to take an indoor cage apart.

Rinse out feeding bowls and drinkers before refilling them. If you use a soap or detergent, rinse it all out before filling with food or water. Overgrowth of algae in the drinking bottle can be scrubbed out with a bottle brush.

Finally, twice a year the cages should be disinfected with a household cleanser.

There are many different kinds of bedding material available. Whichever you choose, be sure to change it on a regular basis. Photo courtesy of Hagen.

FEEDING

Rabbits are vegetarians, that is, *herbivores.* For that reason you have to make sure your rabbit gets the proper food, and does not get sick on foods unsuitable for vegetarians. A rabbit's metabolism requires proteins, carbohydrates, and fats in a definite proportion. In addition, minerals and vitamins are needed, without which an ordered metabolism would not be possible.

The individual nutrient

A sable marten Netherland Dwarf. When feeding your Netherland Dwarf, moderation is the rule of thumb.

requirements depend upon what the rabbit is called upon to do. A pregnant doe and an often used stud buck need more food than your pet dwarf, which you are probably not going to breed. True, a lot of movement requires a greater metabolic output, but the short distances your pet hops are not an unusual expenditure of energy. If, however, you are going to train your dwarf rabbit, then its quantity of food should match its increased work load. Foods for the dwarf rabbit can be classified into several groups:

Enriched Rabbit Feed (Pellets)
Enriched or fortified feeds make up a large group. Every pet shop sells rabbit foods made by various manufacturers. The content of these feeds varies greatly and is formulated for the needs of rabbits. Enriched feeds contain oats (either whole meal or milled as flakes), dry corn, and possibly small amounts of barley and wheat.

These foods are usually in various shapes like rods, bars, or rings. They are mechanically pressed from many ingredients. Besides cereals, pellets also contain grass, molasses (a byproduct of sugar beet or sugar cane processing), vitamins, minerals, and salts. The color varies from light to

A group of Netherland Dwarfs. The activity level of your pet will be a factor in the amount of food the animal consumes.

Pelleted food formulated especially for rabbits is the most important part of a rabbit's diet. Photo courtesy of Hagen.

dark green, depending upon the ingredients. Furthermore, there can be a smaller amount of other ingredients, depending upon the manufacturer: corn, rice, and dried protein compounds. Such mixtures give the dwarf a tasty and varied diet. Dry, these foodstuffs stay edible a long time, although the vitamin content drops (for example, in rolled or milled oats) after more than six weeks of storage. So pay attention to the expiration date usually printed or stamped on the package. If you purchase a pet shop's own mix, which is cheaper, ask how long the vitamin content will stay potent. Although you could still use feed with an expired date, as long as you provide the lost vitamins with supplements, there are other reasons to throw old feed away: moist, moldy, or vermin-infested feed is unusable. Otherwise, the bulk feed from the pet shop's own mix is equivalent to brand name packages from a manufacturer. You can save about 30% to 40% by buying a paper bag full of the pet shop's own mix. Of course, you can mix your own, too. For that, here's a list of the most important ingredients: oats (rolled or whole meal), dry corn kernels, pellets, dried-out wholemeal bread.

If you have several rabbits, or also keep rodents such as guinea pigs, mixing your own feed can be a good idea. The cereals and pellets are for sale at feed stores or country stores. The great advantage of mixing your own is that you can adjust it to your own rabbit's taste. The principle here is the larger the quantity you buy, the less you pay per pound. Consider this possibility, but don't go overboard. It would take a whole horde of animals to eat up a 50-pound sack of rabbit food, and there's also the expiration date to consider, even though the feed is especially durable.

Wholemeal Bread

Hard, dry wholemeal bread can be offered to your rabbit as a dietary supplement. It's made of the same or similar cereals contained in enriched feed. Hard bread gives the rabbit a way to grind down his continually growing incisors. (A rabbit has to work his food over, which is the purpose for all the little angles and corners—hearts, rods, twists, etc.— one sees in prepared feed mix.)

If your pet does not like dry bread, try serving it to him in a mash form by mixing it with water.

Do *not* get the idea of simply giving your rabbit fresh bread. Your rabbit would have digestive problems from which he could even die.

Dry Fodder

Another food consists of fodder, which is dry like the enriched foods, but does not contain as many nutrients. It satisfies not only part of the need for nutrients, but also serves another: its fibrous content is partially undigestible and provides bulk in the rabbit's diet. This bulk is vital to a rabbit, because as a wild rabbit,

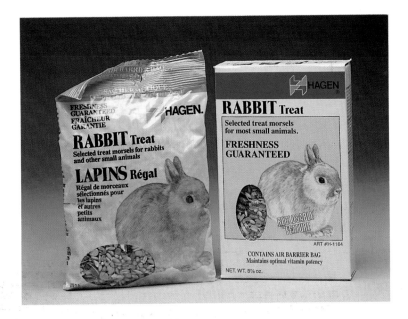

In addition to pelleted feed, pet shops also carry various treat foods. Photo courtesy of Hagen.

**A blue
Netherland
Dwarf rabbit.**

ancestrally, he was accustomed to feeding on enormous quantities of bulk and roughage-rich food in order to satisfy his basic nutritional needs; therefore, his alimentary tract is adapted to a voluminous diet. If you feed your rabbit only enriched rabbit food, that will burden the digestive system by the lack of roughage, which the rabbit can find for himself out in the wild. This dietary error can lead to constipation and tympanites (flatulent colic).

The most important fodder is hay. It's sold in pet shops as meadow hay and consists of dried, mown grass. Other kinds of hay are alfalfa clover (high in protein; use only together with meadow hay), and foliage hay, which, as the name implies, consists of dried leaves.

In addition, edible straw is available from agricultural or feed dealers. This straw consists of the grain stems, and is much more nutritious than hay. As a rule, you should buy feed straw only when it is from oats; other straw is not liked as much.

A bale of hay should be kept in a dry place, which can cause some messiness. So think over well whether you want to buy that much at once. There is hardly a better way to save money, but if only one rabbit eats from it, a bale can last over nine months, taking up space and causing a mess all that time. Here's a tip: if you first put a burlap sack over a new bale of hay, and then cut the bands, you can save yourself a lot of trouble. If the bale is stored at some distance from the rabbit house, you might want to keep only one plastic bag filled with loose hay near the housing. (Once you take off the pressed upper layer of a bale, a whole mess of grass fragments fall out around it.) You can also buy from dealers prepackaged meadow hay to save some work and transportation, but you'll have to pay a lot for it.

Alfalfa can often be obtained from agricultural dealers, but since it should only be fed along with meadow hay or feed straw, it probably is not feasible for your purposes. In any case, hardly anyone is able to store two bales of hay, unless you have the space to keep them dry and store them right near the animals.

You can make your own foliage hay. Spread it out like meadow hay, turned and dried in the sun. It should

An agouti Netherland Dwarf. In this coloration, each hair is alternately barred in light and dark tones, with yellow at the tip.

be fed to the animals only after six weeks of "sweating" time to guarantee that the fermentation process is finished. Make your own hay only if you really enjoy doing it, and only if your rabbit knows how to appreciate the tasty alfalfa hay. Otherwise, the effort for such a small amount is simply too large. That's why you might do better buying ordinary meadow hay.

Fresh Foods

Some rabbit keepers, especially European rabbit keepers, choose to feed their pets fresh foods on a regular basis, a practice which is a matter of personal choice. Just remember that

Your dwarf rabbit's bedding must be changed on a regular basis.

enriched or fortified feed is the key element in a rabbit's diet, as it has been specially formulated for a rabbit's nutritional needs.

The fresh foods, of course, are fed fresh, for they cannot be stored for long. They serve as bulk and roughage. Never feed fresh foods to a rabbit less than six months old.

Fresh food availability depends upon the season. Carrots are the best-known fresh food and are quite readily available. Other advantages of carrots are the long storage time possible (up to a week, which is a long time for fresh vegetables), odorlessness, and a taste which some rabbits find delectable.

My rabbits are enthralled by tiny pieces of cabbage or similar vegetables such as cauliflower, Brussels sprouts, and savory cabbage (placed in their hay holder). They munch up every speck of it. Cabbage

and similar vegetables, unfortunately, have the unpleasant characteristic of smelling somewhat, so I advise you to clean up the toilet corner the very next day after those vegetables are eaten.

There is some controversy as to whether dwarf rabbits can be fed lettuce. It is not advisable, although animals used to fresh vegetables do not get sick from a lettuce leaf.

Every rabbit loves grass, dandelions, and clover. Summer residence in the outdoor enclosure allows the dwarf rabbit to graze in his play meadow for these munchables. If you don't have access to any grounds of your own, you can, of course, pluck the grass for your rabbit. It has to be fed to your rabbit immediately or else spread out in a cool spot. If you give the rabbit grass that's already warm and clumped together, for example, from a lawn mower, you can give him terrible stomach pains. Grass which has already begun to ferment develops

During play periods when your little friend is out of his cage or hutch, he should be constantly supervised.

gases which can inflate your rabbit's tummy and make it hard like a drum or an overfilled balloon. Since your bunny can't throw up, it suffers for hours and can even die of circulatory failure. Also, never feed him wet grass because that has the same effect as fodder which has already started to ferment.

When you go plucking for fodder, be sure the grass, dandelions, etc. are far from the highway or busy streets and from the excreta of other animals, otherwise your rabbit might pick up parasites.

Be alert to your rabbit's strange tastes. Almost all rabbits love to eat tree leaves (which, of course, should not be sprayed), and some of my rabbits don't even stop at rose leaves, which they eat up completely. All rabbits, however, don't get off so easily when they gobble up things. My own rabbits nibbled on a maple leaf without hesitation, which could have had serious consequences. Therefore, be sure to review your botanical knowledge before you bring your bunny any tidbits from your Sunday walk.

Tropical plants are predominantly toxic, but even everyday bushes can be dangerous, too.

Feeding Time and Quantity

Some hobbyists feel that a once-a-day feeding is best (except for pregnant and nursing does, who will probably need more food than this). Others prefer a twice-a-day feeding schedule, morning and evening. Dividing the daily ration into two meals can help to avoid overburdening the rabbit's digestive system. It's quite

A black Netherland Dwarf. Rabbits are notorious nibblers; therefore, make sure that your pet does not have access to any poisonous plant matter.

possible that a particularly greedy little dwarf rabbit can gobble up all his food in a quarter of an hour, and that overloads his stomach. Even if he doesn't get a stomach ache, he'll just sit there all day in front of his empty bowl and be in a bad mood. You can, of course, feed him snacks between meals.

The amount of food to give depends upon the size of the rabbit and the kind of food. Excess food should not be given, for many rabbits will overeat. The result is not a rabbit overflowing with good health, but a fat and possibly short-lived rabbit.

My dwarf rabbits receive a tablespoon of enriched feed with each meal, that is, twice a day. The tablespoon is either level or heaping, depending upon the food value of the feed. In principle, the rabbit should go right to the food bowl and empty it. If, however, the rabbit stands begging all day at the cage screen or if it is difficult lifting him by the neck skin fold, increase the enriched rabbit food. But watch the little beggar carefully; he soon learns that vigorous, heart-rending beggary produces a tidbit. The supposedly undernourished creature can develop into a fat, illness-prone animal who is even too lazy to stand up for food.

In general, overweight is a dangerous condition. Underweight can usually be quickly corrected. If your pet is not interested in even the nicest tidbits, take him to the veterinarian.

The rabbit may often prefer the enriched rabbit food to the dry fodder, so he eats it only after he's eaten his enriched food. That means your rabbit won't overeat the fodder, so you can fill the holder up once a day.

Besides the appropriate fresh vegetables for feeding, there are still other kinds of fresh foods which the rabbit cannot tolerate in large amounts. So try all new fresh foods in very small pieces, fed like snacks. Let your rabbit's taste guide you. If he doesn't like it, then don't use it. Pieces of apple and carrot are delicacies for your rabbit. Think always of the smallest quantity when you feed him unaccustomed foods. A tiny piece of apple tastes heavenly, but if you get soft and give him a whole apple next time, he will likely get very sick.

Because fresh plant food deteriorates very rapidly, ration it out in such a way that all the food is eaten up by the next feeding. You can recognize almost spoiled vegetables by the moist, mushy spots and discoloration in some places. In such a case, remove the bad parts and give your pet the rest that same day. If the food gives off a strong odor or if some mold has already formed, throw it away.

Look out for possibly sprayed or sandy produce, which you have to thoroughly clean and dry before using. If you have to store large quantities of fresh vegetables, store them loosely in a cool place and pick off the rotting spots every day. Fresh food, given with the proper precautions, can be healthy for rabbits.

Drinking Water

Water is an important requirement for your rabbit. A filled half-quart drinking bottle is optimal, for your rabbit can take as much water as he needs from it. Always keep the bottle filled with fresh clean water, except in outdoor cages when freezing weather threatens, at which time give him a bowl of warm water. The mineral water mixes sold for birds are not necessary for properly fed rabbits, and rabbits may not even like that kind of water. My closing tip for this chapter is make sure that newly acquired rabbits use the drinker. You can speed up the process by setting your pet at the drinker and letting some water shoot out of it. After several "lessons," your pet dwarf will begin to drink, which you verify by watching the bubbles rising in the bottle.

CARE

How to Hold and Carry Your Rabbit

The dwarf rabbit is easy to handle. Because of its size and weight, it is quite suitable for being the pet of young, often rather clumsy children who may be helpless in some difficult situations. Despite his small size, the dwarf rabbit is a sturdy little fellow. The flexible spine and long, spring-action legs account for the dwarf rabbit's elasticity.

On the other hand, your rabbit can hurt himself very seriously if he lands in a position in which he can't absorb the shock, such as falling on his back or on his side. This kind of fall often occurs when the rabbit tries to escape an uncomfortable position. Therefore, you should know, first of all, how to hold a rabbit properly.

There are various ways of holding your pet so you can take care of him, carry him and play with him. The simplest and most important grip is the lifting hold, which you will always be using in dealing with your rabbit. It is with this simple method that people make the most mistakes. The first mistake to overcome is the idea that rabbits can be lifted by their ears. I'm rather certain that the owners of authentic dwarf rabbits do not even get the idea of trying to lift their pets by their little two-inch ears, but it must be mentioned for owners of less dwarfish rabbits.

The saying "the longer the ladle, the better to carry it," means nothing but pain and fear for a rabbit. Anyone can understand that. Besides the ears, there are other protruding parts of the body, like the front and rear legs. These are *not* handles, either. Lifting a rabbit by his extremities not only scares him terribly, but can wrench and injure his joints or even his neck.

Lift your rabbit with one of the

All rabbits require regular attention to their ears, but lop-eared rabbits require it even more: their generous earage can be home to a number of pesky parasites.

following methods: either place one hand under the rabbit and steady it with the other hand, or simply pick it up by the neck skin fold.

The second method is better, in my opinion, because the rabbit is calmer and "hangs" more safely. The neck skin fold method is possible with rabbits because they have a loose connective tissue which lends elasticity to the skin there. For this grip, take a "handful of skin" behind the head and lift (but don't let your fingernails dig into the rabbit's skin) until his rear legs leave the ground. Then use your other hand to support the rear part of the body. During all of this, your dwarf remains quite calm because this grip is a forceful one.

When you use the belly lift, however, the rabbit can wriggle around. Therefore, small children and anxious adults should lift by the neck skin fold method. It's more comfortable for the rabbit, too, because its belly is not being pressed. Pregnant does, especially, should only be lifted by the neck skin fold method; this prevents injury

Himalayan Netherland Dwarf. Properly caring for your dwarf rabbit includes providing a nutritious diet and proper housing.

to the unborn rabbits.

To carry your rabbit over long stretches, here are several transportation methods:

The most secure, but also the more uncomfortable (for the rabbit) of the methods is the extended neck skin hold, in which the rabbit is lifted by the neck skin, placed on your crooked or bent arm and held there by the other hand which is still holding the neck skin fold. Every attempt by the rabbit to hop off or to sit up is prevented by the hold on his neck skin fold and the pressure of the rest of that hand on his shoulders. You can also simply carry the rabbit on your crooked arm, but he can jump off or sit up if you don't hold him; he is in danger of a fall unless you keep your eye on him, and the instant he sits up in preparation for a jump, you use your free hand to take his neck skin fold again and pull him back into place. The rabbit shows his fullest confidence in you and how happy he is by stretching out, relaxed, and burrowing his head in the crook or your arm. Just don't clamp his head too tightly in the crook, for he still needs some air.

If your dwarf rabbit gets unruly and self-willed, then use only the neck skin hold (never the ears, remember!) to force him to mind his manners. Take care not to get angry at all with your little rabbit and never strike him.

Nibbling on your clothes or your skin is something your rabbit may do out of boredom, or when looking for something to eat. Nibbling is also a reason why the longer trips should be in a travel cage.

The veterinarian uses the side hold to examine your rabbit, but you shouldn't use it; nor should you use the hypnotic-like position in which the rabbit lies motionless on its back.

For you, an especially important grip is the one that you will use to hold the rabbit still for claw care and abdominal examinations. For that hold, the rabbit sits halfway up, reclines halfway back while being held on your helper's lap. This hold is quite comfortable. Either the seated helper holds the front paws with both hands, or with one hand supports as well as holds the rear legs. In this way, procedures like clipping toenails can be done safely and comfortably.

Claw Trimming

Before I describe this procedure in any detail, which will probably cause you some uncertainty, let me repeat what I wrote earlier: the dwarf rabbit is easy to handle. In this case, it means that the description of this single "difficult" procedure represents almost the totality of care procedures.

Claw trimming is done with a pair of sharp nail scissors or nail clippers. Hold the rabbit's leg and cut the nail to within a few fractions of an inch from the quick (a sensitive portion of the nail which, in pigmented claws, is visible as a red line inside the nail). Be careful not to cut into it. If you do accidentally cut into this sensitive nerve and blood supply—like the root of a living tooth—the rabbit will react violently, and a drop of blood will appear. Disinfect the wound immediately. If it keeps on bleeding, take your wounded rabbit to a veterinarian. However, this kind of wound should not occur if you trim the nail with a properly placed and

deftly done snip. The accident happens because of not knowing how and rushing.

Front claws normally grow faster than the hind ones. Therefore, usually you have to trim only the front nails. That is because in the wild, out in nature, the claws on the front paws wear down faster than the hind ones during all the digging and burrowing the rabbit does, so nature has the front ones grow faster to keep up with the wearing down. Your pet dwarf rabbit can't wear his claws down by burrowing, so the scissors or clippers have to replace the natural wear and tear.

Whatever else is needed for rabbit care will be taken care of by your dwarf rabbit almost entirely by himself.

Fur Care

The rabbit himself carries out his own daily body care, which consists of fur care and cleaning of body openings. All body parts within reach are cleaned and massaged with his tongue. His head is worked over with his paws, the hind ones massaging his

A black Netherland Dwarf. Note the bright clear eyes of this rabbit.

chin, and the forepaws his nose.

Your pet's playful rolling around serves to get rid of loose hairs. During the shedding season is the only time you have to stroke with and against "the grain" (that is, with and against the direction of hair growth) with a small, soft brush.

To cool off your heavily-furred rabbit on hot days, you can lightly mist him with cool water, or simply moisten his ears and paws. It is not advisable, however, to soak the whole creature down, because his undercoat is water-repellent, so the water won't do any good. When outdoor temperatures drop, your rabbit would catch cold because his fur would not dry off. In addition, don't place your rabbit in deep water, either, because, according to my experience, rabbits can't swim. If your rabbit really needs washing off, which often indicates he might be sick, it's better to sponge off the dirty spots with warm water. The important thing here is to dry all wet spots, especially on cold days, to prevent colds.

To help your rabbit perform most of his own hygienic care successfully, he needs a clean roomy cage. Only in that way is it possible for him to keep his big hind paws really clean, which is desirable if you want to cuddle him on your lap. So don't skimp on litter, and do a good job when you clean. Besides, clean litter inspires your rabbit to roll around in it, thus rubbing off loose hairs and keeping himself soft and glossy.

Exercise

An important part of the daily care of your rabbit is exercise. The relationship between nutrition and susceptibility to disease is well known. Chronic lack of exercise causes ills like those caused by overeating. Rabbits lose their good appetite and have to be coaxed with selected goodies to make them eat. They become apathetic and lose their ability to stay active for long before tiring themselves. Extended play periods with your pet can help to prevent or cure this problem. Let the rabbit get some of the action: don't just carry him around. It is best is to let him run around loose in the room or outdoor enclosure, which is, unfortunately, not always possible. Your rabbit should have the opportunity to exercise each day. Playing around with tidbits, cuddling, and movement to reach his feeding station don't count as exercise. Some hobbyists find that offering their pets something to play with promotes exercise. For example, a small container, such as a frozen orange juice concentrate can, makes a fun "toy" that your bunny can chase and roll around.

You may think exercise is not really enjoyable for your rabbit, but if another rabbit gets playful or if he is given a large space to run free, then you'll be surprised to see even the laziest, thickest-furred clown do a few acrobatic leaps and lightning-fast take-offs. Adding other rabbits to your pet's world encourages him to engage in much more activity.

Toilet Training

When your pet has been running around awhile outside of his cage inside your home, a small problem

arises which is not so obvious out in wild nature: the rabbit drops tiny little "pellets" as he runs around, usually after a "warm-up time" of about ten minutes. These little droppings, although rather inoffensive, can be prevented as follows: as your newly acquired pet makes his first exploratory trips around the house, watch him closely. At the first sign of restlessness, vigorous pawing of the ground, or backing up into a corner, pick him up and place him in his toilet corner in the cage. This toilet training is useful, of course, only if the rabbit will be able to climb into his cage by himself after he's trained. That is, is his cage low enough for him to reach the door? If not, perhaps you can set up a kitty litter box somewhere.

However, I must warn you not to expect too much. Not every rabbit can be housebroken, even if you thoroughly and patiently carry out the training properly. Although it's easier to train a doe than a buck, I think that some rabbits are simply incapable of learning to use a toilet corner, or else they just refuse to learn it. It's not a matter of whether the rabbit is male or female, but rather depends on its individual personality and character.

Taking Your Rabbit for a Walk

This section concerns only the leash and harness, which will allow you to take your rabbit for some fresh air outdoors without your having to own or build an enclosure. If you belong to that group of pet owners,

Netherland Dwarf. The smallest member of the dwarf rabbit group, the Netherland should ideally weigh two pounds.

41

then all you need is this "rig" made of leather straps to hitch him up so you can catch him easily. For that, use two cat collars held togther with a connecting ring or band between the two rings of the collars. One collar is closed and slipped loosely over the rabbit's head, and the second passed under the forelegs and over the stomach, then tightened. Attach a leash about one yard long to the ring of this belly strap. All parts of the harness should be of leather and, if possible, padded. The leash should be attached with a light swivel so as to not burden the rabbit unnecessarily. The use of chains or wires is inexcusable cruelty to animals and under no circumstances should they be used. If your rabbit insists on nibbling on his harness rig, you can do nothing but stop using it.

The proper positioning of this harness is important. Leave the neck band loose enough so it doesn't squeeze the throat. Once your rabbit is outfitted with this harness, you can let him graze over unfenced areas; then, when he's strayed too far, he can simply be retrieved. You can't walk him like you do a dog, because he won't understand it and might hurt himself. Even holding the leash is unnecessary and upsets the rabbit. If you insist on trying to pull him on the leash, he will most likely pull backwards, slip out of the belly band, and free himself.

Remember, the harness rig is only for retrieving your rabbit. It might not even be necessary for very calm, serene rabbits. In addition, remember to graze your rabbit far enough away from shrubbery and other possible hiding spots so he doesn't quickly slip away and vanish. Watch, too, so the leash he's pulling along doesn't get caught on a bush or similar obstacle, and pull the harness off. In addition, keep an eye on him, even in an enclosure, and remember he's defenseless when it comes to dogs and other animal enemies, who certainly are not kept away merely by wire screening.

Dangers in the Home and Garden

Dangers really arise only when the pet owner is not watchful. Nothing can really happen to your pet as he grazes around the garden, as long as you stay near him. Dangers at home, however, are quite different than those out in nature. Although a rabbit cannot think as we do, it does have a natural instinct which warns it of danger in the wild. So you can better evaluate dangers the rabbit does *not* recognize instinctively, there are a few hints to remember.

The rabbit does not know about electric wires or other such unnatural (that is, man-made) dangers, but he does know dogs and predatory animals. An electric cord makes a rabbit curious, and since the curiosity is stronger than his fear, he can get into trouble (such as chewing into the cord and electrocuting himself!). You don't have to move all electric cords, but just keep an eye on him without letting him out of sight.

Another danger is open doors, which lead to other, off-limit rooms, or which can slam shut on him as he slips through them. Make sure all doors are closed and all family members know the rabbit is roaming about the room.

Quite another danger is poisonous plants. Green is just about a magical color for rabbits. Often, a rabbit seems to gravitate right to a poisonous plant! Keep all questionable plants out of your rabbit's reach.

A dog or cat can threaten your rabbit. Even when these unlike animals seem to get along together, don't leave them unsupervised. The most peaceable dog and cat still have deep-rooted hunting instincts which can surface in one unattended moment. Our rabbit's only weapon against such a large animal is escape, and that is very limited in a room. Outside, too, the best defense is constant watchfulness. I have been successful with my own rabbits by using the outside enclosure or the harness rig, both of these possibilities allowing some control over the rabbit, yet also providing him fresh air and exercise.

This photo of a Belgian Hare, one of the "standard"-sized rabbits, clearly illustrates the differences in conformation between rabbits of this type and dwarf rabbits.

BEHAVIOR

As we mentioned earlier, your little dwarf rabbit is a descendant of wild rabbits. And although he shows little resemblance to his wild ancestors, there are still amazingly many traits and habits that he has retained from the wild rabbit, a creature who was ideally adapted to the natural environment. He possesses, as a genuine herbivorous gnawing animal (a lagomorph), powerful dental equipment and continually growing

44

Netherland Dwarf. Like people, dwarf rabbits vary in personality.

incisors, which explain his urge to gnaw in order to continuously grind down his teeth to just the right length.

Because the wild rabbit doesn't really have any effective weapons, yet is threatened by a large number of natural enemies, he has to be ready to flee instantly. The wild rabbit's powerful hind legs give him a lightning fast take-off to outrace and outmaneuver his enemies.

The instinctive digging of burrows, too, is only made possible by the continuous regrowth of the forepaw nails which are worn down by

digging. That's why your pet rabbit's forepaw nails often have to be trimmed.

Rabbits have to quickly recognize their different enemies, who hunt in various ways from the ground or from the air, so they can flee the warren in time. The rabbits need highly developed sense organs for that. The most important warning signals are picked up acoustically. A rabbit's upright ears revolve to get a fix on the sound. In addition, the supposedly mute rabbits have a unique acoustic security system. They thump or drum

Himalayan Netherland Dwarf. The more time you spend with your rabbit, the more accustomed he will become to your presence. Some rabbits, in fact, become quite affectionate towards members of their human family.

out short alarm signals with their hindpaws.

These thumps warn other rabbits, who are also listening attentively. If one rabbit takes to flight, the others spring along a few times with him. Your dwarf rabbit, too, will thump when danger threatens, so be aware he's going to suddenly try to hop off.

A rabbit's eyes, by comparison, are only moderately useful. They serve mainly to see threatening movement, which sets a rabbit on edge, ready to flee. Motionless things are scarcely noticed. Watch, the next time you toss a goody into the cage, and you'll see how the rabbit jumps in the direction of the thrown snack, but doesn't see it right away. He sniffs and feels with his nose along the floor of the cage until he locates the goody. This will also help you to understand an occasionally snapping rabbit, who snaps toward a moving object even before he really recognizes what it is.

The rabbit's sense of smell is exceptionally well developed. In addition to using his nose in seeking and selecting food, an action in which your household pet dwarf rabbit has only some instinctive skill, his nose also fulfills social functions. Wild rabbits living in loose association with one another behave in definite ways to facilitate this group living. They leave behind a scent on various objects to tell other rabbits that this is someone's territory. The scent is secreted from a gland under the chin. Both sexes, does as well as bucks, mark their territories like that. A scent, too, notifies the bucks as to which does are receptive to mating.

When two rabbits meet, their mutual sniffing of each other plays an important role. If they cannot identify each other's rank in the local rabbit hierarchy (which would be demonstrated by the submissive animal's making a show of his humility to the dominant animal), they threaten each other. This scenario rarely lasts longer than five or ten seconds. Then either the "scaredycat" or more fearful of the two turns tail and flees (and so is immediately labeled the submissive one), or else the fight starts, with biting, usually to the shoulders. If the attacked one takes up the fight, both rip out large patches of fur from the opponent and circle each other, growling angrily. That is one of the few sounds a rabbit can make. Depending upon the aggressiveness of the two, the encounter can last a few seconds or even a few minutes. If it lasts longer, both contestants can suffer bite wounds in the neck and ears. Fights between two adult bucks who are strangers to each other can be very vicious, and so should be broken up, even if you risk getting bitten yourself in the heat of battle.

The rabbit's sense of touch, too, is interesting. The long whiskers on both sides of the head and nose, as well as over and below the eyes, act like antennae. If you touch those whiskers while the rabbit dozes, he'll suddenly go into a state of alarm. The whiskers help him to keep from bumping into things in the dark.

The Body Language of the Rabbit

The wild rabbit has a well-defined body language to communicate his opinions to other rabbits. The dwarf

Conveniently sized and cuddlesome, these little rabbits can make great pets.

rabbit fully retains this skill.

We've already mentioned the threatening posture, characterized by laid-back ears and tensed body. Normally, however, the dwarf rabbit exhibits a friendly, attentive mood, expressed by his erect ears turning towards the object of interest, and the raising of the forward part of his body.

Your rabbit shows his contentedness and relaxation in his typical position of rest. You can feel the looseness of the muscles when you carry a happy rabbit; he's like a "limp washrag" which fits right on your arm, conforming to all the curves. When exhausted or when it's very hot, the rabbit stretches out on his side, so that he seems much longer and thinner, and pants.

A low-ranking rabbit cringes and lowers his head, his ears laid back flat. This submissive posture is very important for the group life of dwarf rabbits because it protects the lower-ranking ones from constant persecution by the others. If your rabbit strikes a submissive pose when you appear, be especially calm and loving with him for a few days until he regains his self-confidence.

These examples of rabbit behavior demonstrate that a rabbit cannot be judged by human criteria. A rabbit who may snap at you once doesn't have anything against you personally, nor does he joyfully see you as a person every time you show up. You represent for your rabbit, when he is well cared for, a pleasant, interesting being who amuses him, whether with food, outdoor walks, or just some enjoyable petting. If you get along on this basis with your rabbit, you will protect yourself from disappointment caused by too many expectations about his devotion and affection for you.

BREEDING ——————

This chapter is devoted to rabbit breeding. Because this book is not meant for the professional breeder, but for the new owner of one or even two dwarf rabbits, this chapter is short but informative.

One should breed rabbits only if enough time can be devoted to ensure complete and proper care of the youngsters. Young rabbits have to be accustomed to hand and voice as quickly as possible so that, later, they will be suitable for small children, who are the most frequent recipients of these tame, charming rabbits.

The second "risk" associated with

Five-day-old Netherland Dwarfs. Before embarking on a breeding program, consider whether or not you will be able to find good homes for all the youngsters of a litter.

breeding is customers; make sure, before your first breeding efforts, that you will have a reasonably good chance to sell your stock. Only when you've resolved these two questions should you begin the breeding.

The two rabbits sniff and smell each other during the prenuptial meeting. The mating is over when the buck growls. To be sure that the mating is successful, leave the doe with the buck twice.

When the doe becomes pregnant, increase her food rations somewhat from the second week on, and supplement that by putting a calcium and salt spool in the cage.

Gestation time for rabbits is between 28 and 31 days. The litter size is usually between four and six. A nest is always required for housing the young. It should be in a quiet, warm corner of the cage, and you should be able to cover it with a solid wooden box, into the side of which is cut a small doorway.

Put straw and hay into the cage so the doe can build her nest. Then she'll pull out some of her chest and belly fur to finish a nice, warm, and soft nest.

At birth, rabbits are about the size of a pocket matchbox, blind and without fur. In about five days the first downy fuzz grows on the rabbit babies, usually giving a preview of the

For the most successful breeding program, it is best to start out with the best stock possible. This is particularly important if you desire exhibition-quality dwarf rabbits.

fur color which will grow later. Because of their short, round ears and their first fur, they look more like little puppies than rabbits. In ten days the little rabbits open their eyes. Also by this time they are fully covered with downy hair.

Later, the dwarf rabbit babies get their baby fur, which makes them look like tiny balls of wool. One is immediately attracted to them, especially because of their cute round heads and black button eyes.

In about six weeks, the baby rabbits should have been weaned, and are no longer dependent upon their mother. They can switch from milk to regular enriched rabbit food. Babies should

not be separated from their mother because the babies cannot yet produce enough of their own antibodies, which are in the mother's milk. Babies separated too soon from their mother are later more susceptible to disease and do not grow as large as their littermates.

After eight to ten weeks, at the latest, separate the youngsters from one another, because their developing sexuality can easily lead to rivalries.

To guarantee a healthy litter, the doe should be older than seven months, and the buck older than five months. At this age, the body build already usually indicates the sex: the male has a broad head, while the female has a smaller one. After about five to six years, the doe is no longer able to have any more young. The buck, on the other hand, can be bred until old age. If you want to breed just as a hobby, then the doe shouldn't be bred more than once or twice a year.

When mating, always bring the doe to the buck and not the other way around. If you do bring the buck to the doe, she'll defend her territory with tooth and claw. By contrast, the buck doesn't do anything to the doe, for he has other designs on her.

As cute as young bunnies are, breeding them—and properly caring for them—is time-consuming. And keep in mind that within a year you can easily have up to 150 rabbit babies, including grandbabies, from one breeding pair!

Blue silver marten Netherland Dwarf. Breeding for color in rabbits requires a working knowledge of basic genetic principles.

HEALTH

This chapter concerns diseases, their causes and how to cure them. Keep in mind, however, that most diseases arise only because of improper care, and so are easily

4. Improper care
5. Injuries

You can recognize that your rabbit is sick only by observing that he somehow deviates from his normal

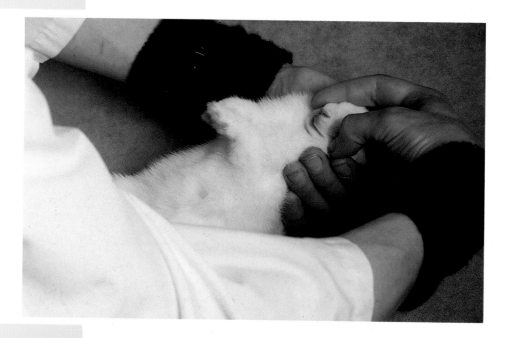

corrected by clean, proper procedures.

The most common diseases or conditions can be classified into five categories:

1. Viral and bacterial diseases
2. Parasite infestation
3. Improper nutrition

appearance. Stiff or dirtied fur, wet or runny nose, and lack of sparkle in his eyes are all reasons for alarm. His behavior, too, can be a sign. A rabbit who likes to eat, hops about, and participates alertly in what's going on around him is seldom ill. Deviation

A rabbit's teeth grow continuously throughout the life of the animal. Therefore, rabbits must be given the opportunity for regular chewing to keep their teeth worn down.

Opposite: A three-week-old baby Netherland Dwarf.

from that pattern can indicate sickness.

Myxomatosis

Myxomatosis is the first disease we'll talk about. It's sometimes called rabbit plague and is transmitted by virus, biting flies or gnats, and green leafy vegetables that have been soiled by wild rabbits. The disease is usually incurable, and the rabbit should be put to sleep to spare him suffering from pain.

Myxomatosis is diagnosed by reddening of the eyelids and skin swellings, often described as "lion head." The rabbit stays very still, sitting around apathetically, his eyes stuck closed. A vaccination is available to prevent the disease. The "plague" usually comes only every several years, but the exact interval cannot be specifically predicted. A

less expensive protection than vaccination against this disease is simply fly screens which keep out the biting flies which transmit the disease. In addition, keep your pet from infecting himself; do not let him sniff around wild rabbit droppings. An infected rabbit must be removed from other rabbits; the disease is called "plague" for good reason—it spreads fast.

Enteritis

A frequently occurring bacterial disease is enteritis, triggered by an overly rich protein diet. Overfeeding and feeding on clover devoid of any hay can also cause this condition. This improper diet disrupts digestion, allowing intestinal bacteria to increase, which adversely affects the intestinal tract. This causes severe pain, and may kill the rabbit.

Treatment consists of switching the diet to good hay and perhaps some chamomile tea. Separate the rabbit from the other rabbits, just as for myxomatosis. Wash your hands after every time you touch the sick rabbit, otherwise you might transmit the disease to the other rabbits.

Coccidiosis

Coccidiosis is an internal parasitic disease caused by protozoa (one-celled organisms), which destroy the intestinal wall. It is transmitted when the rabbit eats soiled feed, thus picking up the disease. The cycle of infection can be broken by frequent cleaning of the cage. Coccidiosis causes severe diarrhea and in many cases damages the liver. The sick rabbit gets very skinny.

To break the infection cycle, clean the cage daily if possible. A veterinarian should make a definite diagnosis, and then he can prescribe medication if needed.

Worms

Several kinds of worms can affect the rabbit's health in varying degrees

A lop-eared dwarf rabbit, known as a Holland Lop.

As far as rabbit illnesses are concerned, preventive care is the wisest course of action. This includes cleaning your pet's housing and his feeding utensils on a regular basis.

owner. They can be prevented by observing a few rules:

1. Avoid sudden changes in the diet.

2. Rabbits always need hay as supplemental roughage or bulk.

3. Fresh clean water must be available at all times.

4. Feed only enough so that the feeding pan is emptied by the next mealtime.

An overloaded stomach is a condition caused by dietary error. Overburdening the muscles in the gastrointestinal tract causes constipation, which is painful for a rabbit, and which can be fatal unless veterinary help is obtained. The symptoms are usually recognizable at once: the rabbit doesn't eat anymore and grits its teeth. Immediate transportation to the veterinarian can save the rabbit's life.

Constipation caused by too much and too highly concentrated feed—that is, feed without any roughage or bulk—is similar to the constipation caused by overloading the stomach and is fatal in severe cases.

Another dangerous gastrointestinal condition is intestinal obstruction. Digestive disturbances and gas cause a hard, ballooned-up abdomen as tight as a drumhead.

Netherland Dwarf. Check your rabbit regularly for any signs of parasitic infestation.

of severity. The rabbit is infected by eating feed contaminated with droppings from another rabbit with worms. Prevention consists of frequent cleaning of the cage.

Skin and Fur Parasites

External parasites are mites, lice, fleas, and, in rare cases, ticks. They cause crusty skin and itching, mainly on the head and rump. The veterinarian can prescribe suitable medicaments to take care of this problem.

Fungus, too, can infect the rabbit's skin. Symptoms are like those described above, and treatment by a veterinarian is absolutely necessary.

Improper Diet

Rabbit dietary problems are primarily caused by inattention and lack of knowledge on the part of the

Improper Care

In this category are conditions

which are caused exclusively by the pet owner. Here, we're speaking mainly to the beginners in rabbit keeping.

Heat stroke is one of these conditions caused by poor care. You've got to know that rabbits can easily tolerate cold down to –4°F, but don't feel so good at a temperature of about 68°F. On hot summer days, absolutely avoid putting your rabbit directly in the sun, or leaving him in a stuffy, warm spot. Otherwise, your rabbit can be brain-damaged and suffer from heat stroke. The rabbit stretches out and pants to ventilate his lungs. If this happens, get him to a cool spot at once and cool off his paws with water. If he doesn't get better very soon (if his breathing doesn't become calmer,) take him to a veterinarian as fast as you can.

Injuries

Our last category includes external injuries. Sometimes they are a result of fights with other rabbits. Homemade cages, if not constructed correctly, can also result in a rabbit's getting injured: the animal can hurt itself on jagged ends of wire and similar dangerous objects. If the wound is small, clean it off and apply a wound ointment. If the wound is severe, carefully transport the rabbit to a veterinarian.

Injured legs should be treated at once because they are constantly in contact with droppings, etc., and open wounds can get infected quickly.

A closing word: remember that many diseases very rarely occur, and that proper care can help prevent their ever occurring. Therefore, it's up to every rabbit owner to have a happy and healthy pet.

A lovely assortment of Netherland Dwarfs. Following the rules of good management can help to ensure the health and contentment of your pet.

INDEX